§§§§§

# The Smuggling Life

## of

# *Gabriel*

# *Tomkins*

Being an account of his Notorious and Felonious Exploits in the counties of Kent & Sussex & Hampshire, and in particular the villages of Mayfield & Hawkhurst, Goudhurst & Wingham, Dungeness & Lydd, Camber & Bulverhythe, Pevensey & Poole, and concerning the towns of Tunbridge Wells, Hastings, Rye, Dartford, Salisbury, Southampton, Chichester, Folkestone, Dover, Sandwich & Margate.

Touching also upon Bedford, Bermondsey, Biddenden, Bletchingly, Breznet, Burwash, Buxted, Canterbury, Cross in Hand, Crowborough, Duddleswell, Dunstable, Eastbourne, Etchingham, Flimwell, Fordingbridge, Godstone, Groombridge, Hadlow Down, Heathfield, Horney Common, Hurst Green, Langney Bridge, Lewes, Maresfield, Pevensey Bay, Rake, Reigate, Robertsbridge, Rowland's Castle, & Shoreham.

The said account having being transcribed, edited and revised by
**Kent Barker Esq.,**
author and journalist of the parish of Benenden.

*To be drowned or be shot*
*Is our natural lot,*
*Why should we, moreover, be hanged in the end-*
*After all our great pains*
*For to dangle in chains*
*As though we were smugglers, not poor honest men?*

Poor Honest Men - Rudyard Kipling

# For Titus

ISBN 978-0-9568421-1-4
Printed by Berforts
© Kent Barker 2011
Published by KBP
Cover design John Belknap
Cover illustration Thomas Bewick, - courtesy of The Natural History Society
of Northumbria, Great North Museum, Hancock.
Maps drawn by Simon Newman

## §§§§§§

So tomorrow I die.

They will take me from this cell. Put a noose around my neck. Run the cart away from beneath my feet. Watch my body perform the hempen jig as it dangles from the scaffold. Will the crowd cheer? Will there be people here at all to see my end? To die in Bedford of all places. No-one knows me here. Now in Kent and Sussex I had some notoriety. There the name of Gabriel Tomkins meant something. Perhaps, it is true, more so five-and-twenty years ago than now. But oh, the ignominy of being gibbeted 'between Hockliffe and Dunstable'. I do not recall ever having visited Hockliffe OR Dunstable. And if my eyes are to be pecked out by birds and my rotting corpse to be held as example to passing children, then surely it could have been in Tunbridge Wells, or Rye, or even Dartford. There, I own, I did some mischief. But Bedford?

So I have perhaps eight or ten hours left. Time enough to contemplate my fate. But scarce time enough to recall all my miscellaneous misdeeds. And it is a curious thing that many are shrouded now in a mist as thick as any that covered the marsh round Romney. Perfect cover for owling. But by God did you need to know your way around. More ditches and dykes and streams than hairs on a man's head. Well, more than the hairs that are left on my head anywise!

3

Through that mist I see the carts laden with fleeces headed for France. Through the fog of time I see the pack-horses groaning under the weight of sacks of tea or half-Anker barrels of brandy on the return journey. I can almost hear the Revenue men riding past in the night. But the memories are patchy now. Was it this night that my brother Edward mistook a turn and ended up with five ponies close tied together in the Rother? Was it that night that Jacob Walter left his piece cocked, stumbled on a stone and near shot his foot off?

And here's the thing. If events can't be remembered back scarce twenty-five years, what will be recalled in a hundred to come? If the ink has faded in a quarter of a century, what will be read after a quarter of a millennium? I go to my death in the year of our Lord Seventeen-Hundred-and-Fifty. What, if anything, will be recalled of my life in the year Two Thousand? By the very nature of my calling little is written in official records. Indeed, you might say that anything written in an official record counts as a failure, for my purpose, during the first part of my career at least, was to be nigh on invisible to the authorities.

It is, you may say, presumptuous in the extreme to expect any to be interested in my deeds (or misdeeds) now, let alone any soul some two hundred and fifty years hence. Yet, should you persevere with this brief account, I think you will own that I have lived a life full of event and adventure. That I managed successfully to ride two horses for so long required some little skill – or if not skill then native cunning. And I have a suspicion that the noble calling of the smuggler will be but a footnote in history and that the real story will die along with me and my kind.

Ah, I hear you about to expostulate, "noble calling indeed, you're no better than a bunch of cut-throats and crooks". But I beg to differ. We preferred to call ourselves free-traders. Individuals prepared to stand up and take direct action against an oppressive state. What, in the name of God, is the logic of making it illegal to export wool? In Yorkshire perhaps. Even in Bedfordshire. But in Kent and Sussex? Just a hop across the channel to the markets of France and Flanders. And likewise explain to me what is the point of taxing Silks and Oils and Tobacco and Brandy, and above all things Tea, so high that none but the richest in the land can afford them? I'm no Leveller, but were His Majesty's Government to cut the taxes by a third, they'd like sell twice as many goods, take increased revenue from them as a result, all but put my profession out of business, and enable even the poorest to afford a cup of tea. But no. Taxes continue to rise from one year to the next to fund foreign wars no-one wants to fight.

But enough. You haven't paid for this pamphlet to hear my rantings and railings. You could have had them for free almost any night after a tankard or two of ale in the *Middle* or the *Oak and Ivy*. And much the same from every man jack to frequent those establishments. For those were notorious smugglers' pubs where plots were hatched, arrangements made and runs commissioned.

So, if we are to return to my tale, I doubt that you'll find much record of my early life. Even I don't know exactly where I was born or if the birth was registered. You see it is likely my parents were unmarried and certainly I never knew my father. My mother struggled to keep a roof over us and bread on the table and made what accommodations she might with such men as would keep her. One lasted longer than others and thus my half-brother Edward appeared. We were thick as thieves from an early age. To be more accurate, we *were* thieves from an early age. Not much mind. Just the odd apple from the Parson's orchard or a pie left carelessly to cool. But we had the run of the town and it soon became clear that Tunbridge Wells, for all its air of respectability, had secrets buried below the surface. Literally below the surface, in the network of tunnels that concealed for a few hours the barrels and bags from a run up from the coast. With the roads so bad it was most common for goods to be carried on pack-horses. And often you'd see six or ten travelling together laden with produce for the market. But when thirty or forty are moving at night chances were they're carrying 'tax-free' goods on their way to London. Everyone knew it happened and everyone closed their eyes to it.

As a young man I was strong and healthy. Indeed even later in life an official proclamation owned I was *"Five Foot Nine or Ten Inches high, ... a very well made Man [with] a very swarthy Complexion, walks very upright, with large dark Eye-brows, which hang over his Eyes".*

I was apprenticed as a bricklayer. It was a good, honest trade though hard work, and we built dwellings throughout the western part of Kent and into eastern Sussex. Before I was twenty I had my master's certificate and found work in the village of Mayfield building a goodly new house for one Mr N...... who wished to move there from Rye. It seemed he was a farmer with sheep down on the Marsh. And it soon became clear that he was able to afford his fancy gables and turrets by selling his wool across the channel rather than nearer to home as the law demanded. Owling, the illegal export of wool, required some planning and not a few men to move the sacks and watch for the Revenue men. Thus it was that Mr N...... recruited me and my brother Edward for a night's work down on the coast by Jew's Gut – a wide open beach between Rye Harbour and Dungeness Point. The work was middling hard. Load the wool sacks onto the pack-horses, wend your way past the ditches and canals and rivers that criss-cross the Marsh thereabouts, collect on the beach, signal to a boat waiting off shore, load the sacks, return the ponies and ride near 30 miles back to Mayfield in time to start work the following day. The only problems were avoiding the Revenue men, and doing all in the complete darkness ... so as to avoid the Revenue men!

Edward and I went on half a dozen owling excursions, learning our way about and proving our worth. But one night we had a scare. As we were heading to the beach we heard horses coming the other way. Only the Revenue were likely to be out at such a time so we tried as we might to hide the ponies. The other riders came close, but instead of cocking muskets and demanding our business, they passed silently by, heading inland with a string of nags staggering under the weight of their burden. It was clear they were carrying untaxed goods *into* the country, where our owling expeditions just *exported* wool out of the land. The hind man, clearly spotting our poor concealment, called out "nice night for it" or some such which I answered in kind as they departed.

Our enterprise prospered and two evenings later I was passing a part of my profit over to the landlord of the *Middle* in exchange for his ale, when a voice behind me declared "nice night for

*Owlers illegally export wool by night*

**Illustration by Paul Hardy**

it", he having recognised my voice from our work on the Marsh Before long we were on the settle by the fire discussing our respective nocturnal activities and it soon became clear that a good deal of effort was being duplicated that might, more profitably, be combined. We had to find horses and men to take the wool to the beach. They had to find horses and men to bring their goods away from the beach. And the boat that brought their goods from France could, as well, be the same one that took ours back over the water. By the end of the evening we had, we were sure, the makings of an Enterprise. All it required was seed money. Our costs were like to be thus: the French goods had to be paid for in advance, the boat had to be chartered and the crew paid. The horses had to be collected and assembled, the wool purchased, baled, loaded and taken to the boat. Then the small kegs or half-Ankers of brandy and pouches of baccy and dollops of tea had to be unloaded off the vessel, put upon the beasts and taken to London to be sold. This meant a three or four night trip, unloading and concealing the cargo before dawn each day, and reloading the same at dusk. It would require payment to the men to accompany the cargo and payment in kind to those as concealed it along the way. But the profits would be huge. Two or three hundred percent. We calculated – in ale admittedly – that we ourselves could make a year's wages in just one run. What could go wrong?

In the cold light of the following morning as I added slaked lime to the mortar and hefted the bricks onto the gantry, it was perfectly clear what was wrong with the plan. Capital. Or the lack of it. There was no possible way we could raise even a portion of the money necessary for such a venture. But at mid-morning when Mr

N... came to inspect the works on his house, I broached the subject with him and he appeared not a little interested. Two days later he informed me he had a group of backers who were prepared to join, and when I had put all the parts of the plan together, I was to meet them to outline the details.

To some surprise I found the organisation of the venture easy to arrange and exceedingly pleasing. I may have been no champion at laying bricks, but with all modesty I can say the planning of the Enterprise was exact in all details. Mr N..... and his group were content. Several had interests in sheep on the marsh so there was no need to find ready money for the wool. The affair passed off just as planned and the profit exceeded my greatest expectation. From that moment I exchanged my trowel for a brace of pistols.

§§§§§

By the nature of the trade we did not shout our doings, so little evidence exists of the early years of what became known as the Mayfield Gang. In reality we were not so much a gang as a loose association of free-traders. If there was wool to export or brandy and tea to import then there were a large number of people I could call on to help out. The Parliament might refer to the runs as 'smuggling', or 'frauds' or 'evil practices', but in those days there was wide support for the trade from almost every quarter in the countryside and on the coast. What man would not wish to earn easy money in one night by escorting goods? What woman would not give shelter to those goods during daylight hours and find feed for the horses and the men if, in return, she is rewarded with monies, lace and a lb or two of tea?

We were an important part of the local economy and had the wholesale support of most of the local community. Later, it is true, some around Hawkhurst went too far and did violence on villagers to keep mouths shut and tongues stayed. But I found that a few shillings or a flask of brandy liberally dispensed was much more effective.

And likewise for the Riding and Revenue Officers. If a bribe would not persuade the man to look the other way, then I found it best to help him off his horse and secure him to a tree or gate while our ponies passed. If it was like to be a cold night I'd spread word at the next farm that there was a soul down the lane who needed some help. In this way I made many friends and but few enemies.

Now you may ask why a Riding Officer would consent to being helped off his horse and tied up when he'd just discovered the very thing his office demanded – to whit a run up from the coast? Well put yourself in his place. He's paid but forty shillings a year from which he has to furnish and feed his own horse. He must ride out most nights in all weathers and if he stumbles on an enterprise what then? He is one man armed with but two pistols and his sword. And as we never travelled with fewer than twenty well-armed men, he is severely outnumbered. Only the very foolish fought back. And they did not last long in their employment!

Of course if the Revenue had prior information about a run – perhaps from spies in France or Holland – they might assemble a larger band of Officers or Dragoons from the local barracks who would outnumber our men. We had then on occasion to abandon the goods and flee. Like as not one of us would follow the horses and observe at which Customs House they were to be secured. Then, next day or the one after, when the guards were down to one or two men, we would call in force and take back our goods and all would be happy. They would have had their seizure and earned their keep, but we would still have our goods albeit after a slight delay and inconvenience.

The most infamous instance of this was some two-year back when I rode with Thomas Kingsmill from the Kentish village of Hawkhurst all along the coast to Dorset with six or seven other fellows. We had been asked by a local outfit to help lay siege to the Customs House at Poole wherein was contained two tons of Tea and thirty-nine casks of Brandy along with some Rum and Coffee. This cargo had been on its way from Guernsey when it was intercepted by the Customs cutter '*Swift*' after a pursuit at sea lasting nigh on seven hours.

We arrived after our long ride at eleven o'clock at night ready for action, but found the Customs House to be guarded by the Revenue vessel moored close by against the harbour wall. However the tide was on the ebb and, as we waited, the ship fell with the water. By two o'clock in the morning their guns were below the parapet and thus we were able to set upon the store with impunity. So the tea at least was retuned to its rightful owners and the entire load of two tons was carried off. It was only through lack of fresh horses that we were forced to leave the brandy and coffee behind. The Customs Service was much displeased with this affair and offered a large reward for our capture.

*Smugglers set upon the Poole Customs House*

On occasion a free-trader would be unlucky enough to be apprehended by a Riding or Revenue Officer and was duly brought before the local Magistrate. It was then that the half-Ankers of brandy left from time to time at that Justice's door would pay for themselves. Many is the time that the case against a free-trader has been dismissed and the Revenue Officer himself has been indicted for false arrest or assault! The Magistrate, you see, is also a part of his local community and knows full well the importance of the trade on the purse of his fellow-villager or towns-man. And, like them, he enjoys his cheap baccy and free brandy, and his wife would be much distressed should she have to pay the taxed rate of five shillings a pound for her tea, instead of the two or three shillings she can generally have it for. Mind though, that this same tea was likely had for six pence a pound in Holland. Thus the Government would force its citizens to pay a thousand-fold markup on the cost price. The free-trader can reduce that price by half and still make a five or six hundred percent profit.

The practice of keeping the authorities sweet and being friend to the local people paid dividends for me in seventeen-seventeen when we were spotted moving a cargo between Cuckmere Haven and Hastings before bringing it inland. We were surprised by a Riding Officer, and much surprised that he persisted in his attempts to apprehend us. One man against twenty is poor odds. Our practice, as I say, was to disarm such lone riders and secure them to a tree or some such whilst we continued upon our business. However this officer, by the name of Gerard Reeves, would not consent to be captured and shots were exchanged. In the melée said Officer Reeves was mortally

14

wounded near Langney Bridge between Eastbourne and Pevensey Bay. The affray was witnessed by some local folk and a warrant then issued for my arrest. That I was later acquitted of the murder of Officer Reeves may be put down to one or more factors. First the witnesses were later unable to say who had fired the fatal shot. This may have been because several shots were fired, or it may have been because these same witnesses had been offered certain pecuniary inducements to be unable to recall seeing who fired the fatal shot. That and the fact that the local magistrate was known to have a powerful thirst, and the Anker of brandy he found upon his doorstep one morning might have helped assuage that dryness of his throat and to have helped him see fit to dismiss the case against me.

Be that as it may, I was duly acquitted but it was, I believe, the first time my name appeared in any official papers. And it was a further four years before it was to do so again.

§§§§§

It never did to use the same route up from the coast too often. One train of pack ponies moving though the night might be overlooked but if it became a regular occurrence then it would enable the authorities to assemble men and plan an ambush. So we would alter our route accordingly, using new safe houses and stopovers on the way. Thus it was that in the first month of the year Seventeen-Hundred-and-Twenty-One, I was to be found at the *Swan Inn* in Reigate. It was a circuitous route into London from Hastings where we had collected the goods, but we had people along the way who were prepared to take some of our cargo, including the landlord of the *Swan* itself. Unfortunately not everyone shared his appreciation of tax-free goods and the Revenue Officers had been alerted and a platoon of Dragoons summoned. We had approached the inn through the cobbled alley at the back rather than coming down the High Street by the old Town Hall. And a good thing too. For the soldiers were waiting in the main thoroughfare. One, hearing the horses, came to investigate and walked into the courtyard through the arch leading from the High Street. He was immediately set upon by our men and surrounded, but managed to let off a shot from his musket before he was overcome. This summoned the rest of the troop and a volley of shots was exchanged. Fortunately they did not think to come round the back of the inn and four of our number were able to hold them off long enough for the rest to make good an escape.

The firing of so many pieces at midnight in the midst of the slumbering town did not go unnoticed, and a loose tongue divulged my name which the Revenue Officers wrote into their report.

We headed east until we reached the village of Bletchingly on the road to Godstone and loosed our animals on Grange Meadow there just before dawn. But the Dragoons were not far behind and another skirmish ensued. Again they fled from our superior numbers and fire-power, but it became clear that, with the authorities thus alerted, we would not make London safe with our load. My brother Edward had noticed that the village boasted no less than five inns or taverns within walking distance of each other, and the landlord of each was soon summoned onto the common. There a quick auction

16

of our goods was conducted and all unloaded and concealed within the hour. The publicans were much pleased, having obtained excellent quality spirits and tea at very considerable discount, and we at least had some cash to show for our venture – though very considerably less than might have prevailed had we made it through to Bermondsey with our goods.

It was to be the start of a year full of incident for your humble author. By the close of Seventeen-Hundred-and-Twenty-One he would be shot and arrested and sentenced to transportation.

§§§§§

*Smugglers land their 'tax-free' goods*

*Illustration by Paul Hardy*

*"They was in a chamber, 6 officers with them,
20 firelocks loaded with powder and ball. At
5 o'clock on Sunday night 9 men well
mounted and as well armed with pistols,
swords, coopers adzes, wood bills and forks,
comes up to ye house, dismounts from their
horses and runs upstairs, firing all ye way.
They wounded 3 officers and got between the
officers and their arms and carried away
Walter and Biggs; if these 9 men had not
carried them off, a 100 more was hard by
ready to make another attack. Jacob Walter
was later recaptured by a commander in the
Queens' Dragoons. The outcome of Thomas
Biggs is unknown."*

So wrote Stanton Blacklocks, innkeeper at the *George* in Lydd, in March Seventeen-Hundred-and-Twenty-One. He described it as the "Battle of Lydd" which is by way of being a bit of an exaggeration, but for a sleepy village on the Marsh it was certainly a piece of high drama. What Master Blacklocks neglects to say is that, of those nine men to effect the rescue, one was shot and wounded by the Excise men, and that one was me.

It all started when Jacob Walter and Thomas Biggs disembarked by Dungeness lighthouse from a French sloop laden to the gunwales with barrels of brandy. 'Twas their misfortune that there to meet them on the pebbly shore were not our men with the ponies, but the King's men with firearms and chains. They must have got intelligence from across the channel that there was a run on, and they managed to outmanoeuvre the rest of our Mayfield mob and get to the landing first. But they knew we were out there on the Marsh somewhere and so, instead of risking the journey to Canterbury with so few men, they put up at the *George* in that village what had once been a fine port before the great storm of Twelve-Hundred-and-Seventy-Eight altered the course of the river Rother and silted up the harbour.

It didn't take long to spread the word, and the innkeeper is right, we soon had upwards of a hundred men at our disposal. But one hundred men are little use in close confined combat. We knew we had to get up the stairs and into the room and disarm the officers and free our men. And ye might well question whether coopers adzes, wood bills and forks would be much use inside – and you'd be right. They would not. But when paraded in the street, below the very window from which the Revenue men observed the scene, along with a mob carrying other farming implements and flaming torches and shouting oaths and obscenities, it was like to put the fear of God into them. Or so I hoped. Anyways you know what happened. We fired a powerful load of ball into the ceiling as we climbed the stairs, again to increase their fear. Then outside the room I shouted to them that they would all die that night unless they released their prisoners, and when they gave no answer we aimed a blunderbuss loaded with buckshot at the door. It fair shattered the wood into a thousand splinters and filled the room with powder smoke. We ran in, each one of us having a pistol in eaither hand – eighteen pieces in all against just six men. Well they were already mighty feared from the outside parade, the racket on the stairs and the blowing in of the door, and they just stood there without offering any further fight. But one of our number, in an excess of enthusiasm, let loose his flintlock, and instead of felling one of the officers, the ball struck me in the arm, causing not a little blood and much discomfort. We later put it about that it was the Revenue who had fired the shot partly to give them some comfort with their superiors when they came to explain how their charges had been so easily released, and partly because I had no wish for folks to think any in our party could not shoot straight. So that was the so-called Battle of Lydd. Quite how Jacob Walter came to be recaptured I cannot say as I was holed up being tended in a friendly farmhouse in Breznet, not far from the village. But that he escaped the gallows or transportation is plain as he was soon riding alongside me again the two of us with a price on our heads.

§§§§§

The next official record of me you are likely to find will be from later that same year concerning my arrest at Nutley, this being a small village in Sussex on the edge of the Ashdown Forest. There is an ancient pack-horse track that leads from there to Duddleswell for travellers bound for Crowborough or on to Tunbridge Wells. It's wild and remote country and so was perfect for our purposes and, being not far from Mayfield, those that did live thereabouts were generally known to us and sympathetic to our cause.

The Revenue, either still irked at what had occurred at Lydd, or just more vigilant than usual, were lying in wait for us at Burwash in such considerable numbers that to fight them off was impossible. Flight was the only option and we had to abandon our cargo and spur our horses to a gallop. Usually such a chase would last five or ten miles before the Revenue men would lose heart and return to their Customs House or Barracks. But not on this occasion. Past the common at Burwash we hastened, through Broad Oak, Heathfield and Cross in Hand, but still they pursued us. Now we had the choice of turning north-east towards Mayfield itself, or north-west towards Maresfield. A quick discussion ensued at the junction of the roads, and most felt it imprudent to lead the law officers into our own village where quantities of untaxed goods were stored in cellars and barns, even though we ourselves might have found concealment there. So we set forth for Hadlow Down and Buxted, thinking that when we reached Nutley we could turn back east along the lane and lose our pursuers in the forest.

Unfortunately for us one of their number also knew the byways in that part of the countryside and they split forces at Horney Common with half their number following up through Fairwarp to Duddleswell and thence turning back towards Nutley. Meanwhile we were at Nutley turning off along the lane towards Duddleswell. We were caught in a classic trap with Officers both before and behind us, and in the deepest part of the sunken track with no ready means of escape on either side. There was nothing to do but surrender though such a course was most abhorrent to our nature.

The Revenue put it about that I turned King's evidence in return for a lighter sentence and early release. But it is not true. At the Lewes Assizes I was sentenced to seven years' transportation and eventually shipped off to the American Colonies at New Providence. Many have written of the harsh vicissitudes of the voyage across the

Atlantic sea and the work of an enforced labourer on the tobacco plantations and I will not tire you with the details here. Suffice it to say that the irony was not lost on me that the commodity I was now producing with the toil of my hands in order to profit the Crown from the taxes levied on it, was the very same as I had oft brought ashore at Fairlight or Dungeness in order to let the people have it untaxed!

Life on the plantation was not too incommodious and I made common cause with those colonists who also railed against the burdensome taxes imposed upon them. My sentence still had several years to run when I decided I'd enough of the New World and pined for the Old. Thus in Seventeen-Twenty-Four I effected an escape to the Island of Cuba and from there found passage home on board the British Man o' War *Happy*. You may wonder why a Captain in the Royal Navy might be prepared to convey an escaped criminal back across the Atlantic, but he'd lost some of his crew to scurvy and a few who had jumped ship on seeing the turquoise waters of the Caribbean, and so was desperate for all manpower he could muster.

Back in England I went under the name of Kitt Jarvis. As an escaped convict I faced the death penalty if apprehended, and could find no lawful employment. I settled first in London and thence looked to resume my calling as a free-trader. But, following the incident at Nutley, our Mayfield group had disbanded and, instead of organising the runs myself, I was forced to work as a hired hand for the enterprises of others. Jacob Walter was still in the business and we oft times rode together for the Hawkhurst or Groombridge outfits until a law officer spotted us on one run and had a price of one hundred pounds put upon our heads.

23

My fortunes turned again in Seventeen-Twenty-Eight when we were carrying north from the coast some considerable quantities of brandy shipped from France on board a collier and thence transferred to smaller vessels and landed at Pevensey.

We had just reached the town of Battle when we were accosted by Revenue Officers and a considerable skirmish ensued. Many pistols were discharged and muskets too. Swords and cutlasses were brandished. Some of our number made good their escape with the bulk of the goods but I, alas, was captured and held at gunpoint and marched off to gaol. And there I languished to await my fate. Past were the days when others from our group would attempt a rescue, and the judges in Canterbury were not as amenable to a bribe as their colleagues in Lewes were wont to be. Like as not I would be staring straight at a noose for it had become the policy of the Government to show no mercy to us free-traders.

There was, however, one certain way to gain a pardon and that was by turning King's evidence and providing copious details of our exploits to the authorities. This was not so much of a betrayal as it might sound, for it was common to tell tales of runs long past and to name men long dead, or gone to live abroad, or to give them fake names and swear that those were the names they went by on a run.

Thus, once more I escaped the gallows and was told that I would, again, find myself a free man should I but give evidence to a Parliamentary enquiry that was being convened to consider corruption within the Customs Service.

My evidence to the Committee headed by Sir John Cope is a public record and can readily be discovered. But I think it worth here adding a few footnotes to aid clarity. Much of what I relayed, about the landings had happened long in the past. Indeed I was, as Sir John said:

> *"... used to hire vessels to go over into Zealand, to buy tea and other goods there, which he and his confederates used to land on the coast of Kent and Sussex, in the night-time, which goods they always conveyed to London, in companies of ten or twelve armed men; that they travelled in the night-time, and generally lodged their goods five or six miles out of town, in houses hired for that purpose, and then brought them up 100lb.or 200lb. weight at a time, in the night, or at breaking up of the watch."*

But that was ancient history. It is true I had, for some while since my return from the Colonies, been involved in the disposing of the goods to "grocers and druggists" in the capital and that the *Saracen's Head* in Carter Lane was a favourite dropping-off point. This was a destination for carriers from throughout the south of England and, with the four main taverns - *Saracen's Head, White Horse, The Bell,* and *The Rising Sun* all adjacent to each other – there was so much coming and going of legitimate goods at all hours of the day and night that a few extra Ankers or sacks would hardly be noticed.

I was, however, a touch malevolent in exaggerating the quantities of goods that we were wont to move. For I told the Committee that in one year we imported, transported and sold on *"15-20,000 lbs of tea or coffee."* I could scarce credit that they believed so extraordinary a tale, but they did, and then they came to wondering what might have become of that part of the cargo that should have been seized by the Customs! In general the Revenue men calculated that they apprehended between one-tenth and one-twelfth of the goods landed. Indeed we would, from time to time, ensure that they did so – by leaving a cache of tobacco or tea in a place easy for them to discover so they could justify their employment. This system was also designed to dissuade the Government from passing yet more onerous laws or employing yet more Excise men to combat our efforts.

The result, however, of my evidence was to make the Cope Committee question where the ten or fifteen percent of all that tea I claimed to have brought in, had gone. And they were, of course, led to the conclusion that the Customs men themselves were spiriting it away and selling it on the illicit market to their own profit.

This, of course, was wont to happen in a small way. But Sir John Cope became convinced that it was a large and widespread practice and, accordingly, he recommended the dismissal of copious persons employed by that Service. Thirty Officers were removed from the Customs outright. Nigh on four hundred others were suspected and questioned, of those more than one-fourth admitted some malfeasance and, if I recall rightly, around forty-five were compounded for their offences.

This, as you may imagine, left the Revenue Service in a parlous state with far too few men to carry out their duties and thus they immediately set about recruiting new Riders.

18th century British sloop as used by the
Revenue Services to combat smuggling

*Illustration by Kevin Crisman courtesy of Lake Champlain Maritime Museum*

There has been much speculation by them as knows me as to why I should have put my name forward for one of those vacant Riders' posts. Some said it was solely to save my own miserable hide, others held that I was a cowardly turncoat intent on betraying my former friends and comrades.

The second assertion is absolutely false and although there is some truth in the first, it is not the whole truth. To understand my motives you must first consider the progress of my career. As a bricklayer I made but paltry money. As an Owler I earned more but spent it quickly. As leader of the operations in Mayfield over those years between seventeen hundred and seventeen and seventeen twenty-one, I made, it is true, a small fortune. But the bulk of that money had now been spent and there I am, lately turned forty years old, with no visible means of support. After three arrests, one deportation and a spell in gaol, returning to my old occupation was simply not an option. Sir John Cope told me as much after I had spoken to his enquiry. "Tomkins," he said, "you are a marked man. Should you return to your previous ways only the hangman's noose awaits you." It was sobering advice.

Thus I conceived a plan whereby I should have some outward sign of honest employment and yet be able to supplement my income along the way. And what better method to do it than by becoming a Riding Officer for the Revenue Service of the Government of his Majesty good King George II?

I had, in the past, been somewhat dismissive of Riding Officers. But now I knew better how to play the game. You patrol for an hour or two at dusk each evening. If the weather is particularly inclement you retire to a local inn where, generally, there are those present who will buy you ale or brandy in order to ensure that you sit tight in the one place and forget anything you might have overheard being discussed. But I took the employment one stage further. If I knew or suspected that a run was being planned on my patch I would inform my masters who might furnish me with assistance. In which case I would casually let drop in the inn the night before that there was to be a group of us riding out as we suspected a landing at such and such a beach. Then the next night, on patrol with six or ten fellow officers, we might spy a beacon burning on that beach and ride in all haste towards it. When we arrived there we would invariably be too late for the activity, but might find a small cache of sacks or casks in the dunes. These we would take back to the Customs House and write a report saying as to how we had but narrowly missed the landing, but had captured a goodly quantity of untaxed goods. Meanwhile, of course, a few miles down the coast the real landing would have taken place safe in the knowledge that the Riding and Revenue Officers were elsewhere engaged.

Thuswise, as the fox in charge of the hen house, I prospered in my new career and would often find small gifts left for me should I happen to mention that my household was running low on tea, or that my cellar was nearly dry. And if I suspected that a big run had taken place, I might casually drop into the conversation that I had was short of ready cash and my account at this or that shop was overdue. And lo and behold, by the following day the debt had mysteriously disappeared!

Of course, from time to time it was necessary actually to make an arrest to show how assiduously I was pursuing my job. And this too could be done with a nod and a wink. In the bar I might let drop that the Revenue Service was like to make a special investigation of this or that area as so few villains had been brought to book. Then a night or two later I would come across two persons escorting a string of laden ponies. They would discharge their pieces into the air and submit to being arrested. And then, later, the Magistrate would throw out the charges on a technicality and everyone would be happy. Just occasionally people from outside the area would come in and try to take a piece of the action without paying their dues to the locals. This was considered bad manners and, should it persist, I would get to hear of it and they would be duly arrested. I would get the credit for bringing them to justice while the local free-traders would have had the competition removed without having to resort to violence on their own behalf.

So, as you can see, my new employment worked to everyone's advantage, and though some treated me with suspicion and disdain, most people were prepared to greet me in the street, pass the time of day with me and to stand me drinks at the inn. It is true that this was but a poor substitute for the genuine camaraderie and friendship we had enjoyed in the old days in Mayfield, but times change and needs must.

That I was successful in my new calling can be judged by my rapid preferment. Within months of my appointment as Riding Officer I was offered the post of Customs Officer in Dartford and

30

Surveyor of the Dartford Riding Officers and then, shortly thereafter, I was appointed Bailiff to the Sheriff of Sussex.

Now you might wonder, given the state of the roads, how it could be possible to combine all these roles. And the truth of the matter is that it wasn't possible. If I was in Dartford I could not be in Sussex save for a journey of a day or more. If I was riding out along the coast of a night, I could be in neither Dartford nor Sussex the next day. But each post paid a modest salary and, along with the various inducements I have referred to previously, I was making a goodly sum.

Perhaps, in hindsight, pursuing the job in Sussex was a mistake for it took me back to my old haunts where I was known by many and, in that, known as a law breaker rather than a law enforcer. There are not many that actively like the gamekeeper who was used to be a poacher. In Dartford I was all but unknown and could carry out my business at the Customs House with little other than the usual animosity for anyone holding such a post. But in the towns and villages of Sussex it was a different matter.

Thus, when I was dispatched to Rye to arrest a certain Thomas Moore, my decision to put up at the *Mermaid Inn* was perhaps unwise, this being a notorious smugglers' haunt. Indeed I remember back in the twenties we would carouse the night away in the bar of that inn with pistols drawn and on the table in front of us and no man dared question us.

In my defence I can argue that the *Mermaid* was but next door to the Customs House in the town and thus lodging there was convenient for my work. But since the landlord was known to be sympathetic to all free-traders I was not accorded much of a welcome.

Anywise I arrived and duly sought out and arrested said Master Moore and conveyed him to the Ypres goal and thence to the court. But the Magistrate was clearly partial to a drop of untaxed brandy for he immediately let the prisoner out on bail.

That evening I thought it prudent to dine in my chamber, but had not got beyond a brace of lamb chops when there was some commotion in the corridor outside.

The door was stout and was locked so I was not much afeared, but the Landlord had another key and on an instant opened my door to Master Moore and his associates.

Looking back I do see the irony of the situation. It was not so many years hence that I and other men from Mayfield had sprung Jacob Walter and Thomas Biggs from the *George Inn* in Lydd. Now here was I in a similar position in Rye, but this time it was I who was the Revenue man, on the wrong side of half a dozen smugglers' flintlocks.

They fair ransacked my room and grabbed what papers they could find pertaining to the bond that had been put up as bail for Master Moore. Then they grabbed me and frogmarched me out of the town down to the salt marsh where they proposed to drown me. Upon my pointing out that this would certainly be a capital offence, wiser counsel prevailed and they escorted me down to the harbour. The tide was on the rise and it seemed certain I was to be taken across to France and abandoned there. With no money and little knowledge of the local language, returning to England would be no simple matter.

I was bound and flung into the bows of a small lugger. I noted she was a typical smugglers' vessel, gaff-rigged for extra sail area, and her hull carvel-built, that's to say with every plank close-butted to the next rather than clinker built with the planks overlapping. This again was done for speed and meant that she would be able to outrun a Revenue cutter, which was like to be bad news for me. But what she couldn't do was put to sea if tide and wind were against her. As the sea had receded over the centuries it had left the town of Rye an isolated inland hill, so the channel from the town's harbour to the open water out by Camber Sands became ever longer. The passage was formed by the estuaries of the three rivers – Rother, Brede and Tillingham – and so narrow that no boat could tack along it if the wind were southerly and onshore. With the tide on the ebb a boat could drift down and out to sea but it was nigh on impossible if the tide was coming in. But that's the time when a boat could enter the harbour, and to my delight I spied the *Amelia* – the Rye Customs' sloop - nosing up the channel. I was immediately gagged and hidden under a quantity of sail but the Commander of the Revenue vessel, Nathaniel Pigram, did his job well and searched all in the harbour diligently. Where he'd expected to find a barrel of brandy or a sack of tea he eventually discovered your humble servant at the bottom of the lugger, smelling of tar and salt. It was a narrow escape and taught me to be more circumspect in my dealings with the people of Sussex.

*Revenue Officers flee Smugglers at Rye*

**Illustration by Paul Hardy**

While it may have been prudent for my health to stay in Dartford, it was not so efficacious for my pocket and, by the following year, without any earnings from my bailiff's work in Sussex, my outgoings were beginning to exceed my income. I even petitioned the Treasury in the summer of Seventeen-Thirty-Six in an attempt to increase my share of any seizures of monies or goods that I made. This petition they dismissed, upon which I had no option but to take it on myself to increase this portion unilaterally. This meant holding back a part of any seizure and finding a market for it myself. This was a risky undertaking as one might chance buying untaxed goods from a free-trader, but not from a Customs Officer!

So I employed others to assist me. When Bexhill Riding Officers arrested Thomas Black in February 1737 they noted that he *"rode about the country with arms and made seizures pretending to be a Customs Officer ...under the protection and encouragement of Mr Tomkins ... surveyor at Dartford."* Another 'assistant' was Henry Geale. A year or two previously he'd been involved in the shooting of Mr Bilson at Lewisham and his defence was that he was working for me as a Sheriff's Officer at the time. Though the jury at Maidstone convicted him of Bilson's murder, he was later pardoned since he was technically in Government employment at the time. As the Customs' solicitor noted: *"Tomkins's companion was one Geale and has a rather worse character than Tomkins."*

The evidence of an informer calling himself Goring did little to advance my cause. He accused me of continuing to do business with my old comrade, Jacob Walter, for much of the time I was

35

employed by the Revenue. In his deposition about a confrontation between the Groombridge Gang and the Revenue at Bulverhythe he asserted: *"Mr Tompkin was allway as most people know, a villain when a smuggler and likewise officer."*

By 1741 it seemed the full extent of my double-dealing was about to be discovered and I had to leave Dartford and my employment in a hurry late one night. My job prospects were decreasing. I could no longer hunt with the hounds, and reverting to my former life running with the hare was becoming more and more difficult. But after a brief sojourn in London, I did return to my former stamping grounds along the Kent and Sussex border, and would oft times be found in the bar at the *Oak & Ivy* in Four Throws, outside the village of Hawkhurst. If you'd called for Gabriel Tomkins you'd have received no reply, but if you sought out Joseph Rawlins I'd like as not have answered you. At this time in the early 1740s a group of free-traders were operating from this inn and they became known and feared over a wide area as the Hawkhurst Gang.

§§§§§

The Hawkhurst men had acquired for themselves a fearsome reputation for violence not just against the Government forces, but also against possible informers among the general populous.

That the reputation was justified cannot be doubted, but it is perhaps worth remembering that the trade had changed mightily since I was running the Mayfield men twenty years previous.

In Seventeen-Thirty-Six the Parliament passed the legislation known as the *Act of Indemnity for Smugglers.* At first examination this seemed like good news. Any smuggler, even one being held in custody, could henceforth obtain a free pardon for all his offences if he confessed them all and swore the names of his associates. However, if he should return to his old ways, why then he could be tried for all those old offences previously pardoned, plus any new ones, and would thus be the more likely to face the gallows rather than being transported. The law also imposed the death penalty for simply 'hindering' a Revenue Officer, and soon it was likewise punishable to 'assemble for the purposes of running contraband'.

Should information be laid against one suspected of smuggling then his name would be '*Gazetted*' and he had forty days to surrender to the authorities. If he failed to do so he was guilty of a capital offence. Now this was a most pernicious law as you can imagine. The reward for informing on a suspected smuggler was raised to £500 – a king's ransom for most working people. So labourer John but mentions my name to a Revenue Officer to collect his monies, and it is published in the *Gazette*. Then what should I do? If I fail to turn myself in I face being 'turned off' on the gallows. If I do give myself in I likewise face being turned off if convicted of merely assembling or hindering. Much the best course of action would be to ensure that labourer John does not inform on me. And for that I might pay him a visit in the night and hold a knife to the throat of his wife or children. If he's farmer John then I might set light to a small rick in his yard and let him know that the full barn could just as easily go up. In other words the new laws provided compelling incentives for the free-trader to take a very different approach to local people. Where, in my time, a half sovereign or bag of tea would suffice to still loose tongues, now direct threats to life and limb are the order of the day. Not that I condone the actions that made the Hawkhurst mob so infamous. But I believe in part it was the Government themselves what created the situation that made them possible, or even inevitable.

The nature of the business had also changed in the way different outfits worked together. There had always been a degree of co-operation between the people of various villages to finance the runs and to unload and transport the goods. But now the penalties were harsher, there was greater incentive to put on a show of force to frighten off or discourage the Revenue.

Thus, in Seventeen-Forty-Four or thereabouts, when three cutters had unloaded their untaxed goods at Pevensey near Eastbourne, we assembled near five hundred pack-horses to transport the merchandise inland. Getting so many animals and men together at one time and in one place was no mean feat in itself, but the sheer show of numbers was enough to discourage any Customs Officers or even a platoon or two of Dragoons.

And, if they were not sufficiently discouraged by the numbers, then they were like to be by greater aggression that we had been wont to use previously. Later, in December that same year, two leaders of the Hawkhurst outfit were taken at Shoreham and committed to jail. The news came back to the village and, within a few hours, a large mob had been assembled and rode to Shoreham to release them. In broad daylight they entered the town with cutlasses drawn and firing shots into the air. They discovered the Customs men in a house where they were drinking and took three of them bound neck and heels and set out back to Hawkhurst threatening to broil them alive. They released one Officer when they had gone but five miles but the other two they took to a wood near Hawkhurst, stripped them naked and bound them to two trees. There they whipped them near to death, scorched them with fire and finally conveyed them back to the coast to be put aboard a ship for the Continent. Since England was presently at war with France regarding some treaty with Austria over who should succeed the Hapsburg throne, it is very likely that two officers of the English Crown would be immediately apprehended when they set foot on French soil and hanged or shot as spies.

I was not riding with the Hawkhurst men all the time, having other business to attend to in the south of London concerning the distribution of the goods lately arrived from the coast. Thus I was not privy to all the manifest and scurrilous deeds carried out by Arthur Grey then their leader. He had amassed such a fortune through the trade in uncustomed goods that he built for himself a mansion, Seacox Heath, close by Flimwell, which contained its own concealed warehouse for the goods. (I never did discover whether it echoed the name of 'Seacocks' which was given to the free-traders of Hawkhurst, or whether they were termed Seacocks after Grey's house.)

Arthur was already a legend from north Kent across to Hampshire largely for his part in the killing of Customs Officer, Thomas Carswell. As I recall it started on Christmas Day itself at the end of the year Seventeen-Forty. Grey's men landed a quantity of tea – some fifteen hundredweight – on the beach between Hastings and Bulverhythe. They carried it on thirteen or fourteen horses to a barn near Hurst Green on the main road up to London and retired to an inn for refreshment and celebration. They had thought that, because of the season, there would be no Revenue Officers around and thus one of their number, who went by the name of Trip, was mightily surprised to be awoken by the sound of both officers and soldiers trotting past in the moonlight. He immediately raised the alarm and rode round the villages thereabouts collecting together men and arms.

When some thirty assembled at the barn at Etchingham, their worst fears were realised: the tea had been discovered and taken by the law officers. Despite the cold, Arthur Grey made his gang strip to their shirts and swear an oath of damnation to anyone who left before the goods were recovered.

Thus the angry men set off after their tea and came upon the wagon on which it was loaded at Silver Hill nearby, before the descent to Robertsbridge. They overtook the cart forcing it to stop by firing their pistols and muskets. Officer Carswell fell dead, and a dragoon was severely wounded. The other soldiers were captured, the tea recovered and distributed among the men, one of whom, John Boxhall, later turned King's evidence and helped to send Grey to the gallows for his part in the night's activities.

But that was not before Arthur had stamped his vicious mark on the business and on the local population. Not for him the gentle word and the distribution of a few shilling here and a half-Anker there to keep people quiet. No. He was wont to shout at, threaten and beat neighbours if he thought they might talk.

*Celebrating a successful 'run'*

**Illustration by Paul Hardy**

To further intimidate them Grey would seize itinerants passing though his village and serve them most cruelly. One peddler named Lyon was barbarously cut and mangled by Grey and another, a Laceman, was attacked on the road and his property and money stolen.

And that was as nothing to his dealings with fellow free-traders with whom he fell out. In April of Seventeen-Forty-Six or thereabouts, Grey entered into an agreement with the men of Wingham – a village between Canterbury and Sandwich – as well as those of Folkestone, to bring in a goodly quantity of tea, some twelve tons, off the *Old Molly* in Sandwich Bay. This was not, in my humble view, an overly clever location, as the bay is exceeding wide and open to view on all sides, while there are barracks full of soldiers at Dover, along with copious Customs and Revenue Officers, and down a straight road at Canterbury there's an Assize just waiting to impeach miscreants. Anyhow, that was the location chosen and Arthur asked me to come along and would hear nothing against the plan.

Events unfolded thuswise: our men from Hawkhurst with others from Sussex joined those from Wingham and Folkestone – nigh on two hundred all told - and assembled at Sandwich Bay with some three hundred and fifty horses to unload the cargo. Grey had sworn an oath with the others that none should leave the beach until the job was completed. The Revenue was alert to proceedings and kept us under surveillance from a safe distance. Since there were only eighteen Revenue Officers under the command of the Margate Tide

Surveyor, Gervase Cowper, we were not much concerned, knowing that so small a force would not try to impede our superior numbers.

So the *Old Molly* came inshore and her cargo was unshipped and loaded onto the pack-horses. But twelve ton of tea takes a time to remove, and the local men began to move away with their loads before we had got ours onto shore. Meantime Master Cowper had sought out some country people better armed than his Revenue Officers and, when he saw the Wingham and Folkestone men move off, he marched along the beach to challenge us.

We drew up twelve in a rank and discharged sixty or seventy pieces at them, but we were on open ground and under fire from them ourselves. Eventually we had to abandon the remainder of our cargo and ride off – some of us two or three to a horse.

Grey was, as might be imagined, incandescent with fury. He sent to the Wingham group demanding that they share out their part of the haul, but this was refused. He then threatened to attack the Customs House at Margate where 'his' teas would like to be stored. But we had intelligence that Cowper had send to Canterbury for re-enforcements and had asked a naval officer to put a party ashore at Margate to protect the goods they had seized. Arthur then summoned me and Jeremiah Curtis and dispatched us back to Hawkhurst post-haste for re-enforcements.

We rode all through the night, and by the following morning were back in Wingham with nigh on a hundred men. We had with us a selection of Fuzees – long muskets – and pistols, but relied mainly on our broad swords for the fighting that ensued. It was a battle of some considerable intensity up and down the main street of the village, with

43

women and children and honest citizens fleeing before us and sheltering in their houses afeared for their lives. We failed to find the tea, but seven of their number were wounded, two considerably, and in the end we made off with some forty horses belonging to them. Grey no doubt accounted it a good morning's work but of course it made mortal enemies of the men from Wingham and Folkestone and meant that none from Hawkhurst or Sussex could again do business on the shores of that part of Kent.

Arthur didn't remain leader much longer after that. He'd been sailing too close to the wind for some while and was now arrested mainly for his part in the killing of officer Thomas Carswell at Hurst Green. Though the actual charge that sent him to the gallows was *"Aiding and assisting in the running, landing, and carrying away uncustomed Goods" at Lydd on 13th Day of August 1746."*

Before his death, the pastor at Newgate prison recorded that:

> *"He has shewn the most unchristian-like and devilish Behaviour... 'tis on all Hands agreed, that this unhappy Wretch has been most infamous: and acknowledg'd in the general, that he had been a very dissolute and wicked Man".*

Arthur was but thirty-four years old when he went to meet his maker on Tyburn Hill. Before turning to smuggling he'd been apprenticed to a butcher. Some said he'd never changed his trade.

§§§§§

*The gibbet at Tyburn Hill where*
*Arthur Grey was executed*

If anything, the man who succeeded Arthur Grey as leader at Hawkhurst, might be accounted even more devilish than his predecessor. Certainly if injudicious behaviour and sheer arrogance were to be the benchmark, Thomas Kingsmill would have won the contest hands down. He and his brother George hailed from Goudhurst and had so afrighted the citizens thereabouts that the townspeople formed a local militia to defend themselves from the Hawkhurst men who made so free with their horses and goods.

Tales of the misdeeds of Kingsmill and his men had become legend in the area: houses rifled, pockets picked, property set on fire and lives taken. It was not uncommon for members of the gang to arrive at an outlying farmhouse at midnight, wake the inhabitants and demand a fully cooked meal of the best ingredients. When one farmer's daughter, a maid of unsurpassed beauty, refused the suit of one of Kingsmill's followers she was set upon, violated, assassinated, and her body found in a mutilated state too awful to look upon. Other farmers' wives and daughters were set upon on their way to market, stripped and bound in a state of nudity to posts or trees and then pelted with their own butter and eggs just for sport.

One military man, George Sturt, had lately returned to the village having been honourably discharged from his regiment, and found the Goudhurst folk debating as to whether they might leave the area altogether to escape the terrors.

Sturt urged them to fight back, sent for arms, powder and ball, and held training sessions up by the church in the use of fusil and flintlock.

46

News of this audacity reached 'Staymaker' Kingsmill who ordered his men to capture one of the militia and torture him until he gave up details of the village's defenses. This the poor man did readily and, doubtless to his considerable surprise, he was released and sent back to give 'General' Sturt a message: on April 20 Seventeen-Forty-Seven the Hawkhurst men would march upon Goudhurst, take the village, kill all therein and burn it to the ground!

As a method of putting the fear of God into their hearts this was surely a bold and clever move. As a tactic before a battle, however, it had the disadvantage of letting the enemy know in detail just what were the invaders' plans. And, instead of confusing them by attacking a day early, or even delaying the assault until the 21 or even 22 April, Master Kingsmill abided resolutely by the letter of his threat.

And, if this were not foolish enough, he ignored suggestions from many at the *Oak & Ivy* including myself, that he might attack on two or more fronts, or form a diversion to lure the defenders away from their posts. With commendable courage but, as it proved, lamentable judgement, he determined on a full frontal assault from along the Biddenden Road.

'General' Sturt meanwhile had been organising his defences. Trenches had been dug around the Church, and positions re-enforced. Snipers were set in the bell tower and other upper windows. If you know Goudhurst at all you will recall that the entrance to the village from the east narrows mightily where Church Road meets the High Street and travelers have to negotiate a tight double bend by the lych gate. The only other way into the village from

47

that direction is by way of Backlane, but this had been so well blocked and fortified as to make it impassable.

But, in all likelihood, that mattered not as Kingsmill was determined to ride into the town direct with such a show of force that none would in future gainsay or oppose him. There was a brief parlay on the outskirts but the Staymaker contemptuously dismissed a demand that he surrender and threatened to dine on the very hearts of the villagers after the battle was won.

Accounts vary as to how many Seacocks took part that day, but it cannot have been less than a dozen and was probably some twenty or more. They spread out across the street and rode into the village, doubtless looking forward to ale in the *Star and Garter* once the fun was over. Imagine their surprise, therefore, when the Goudhurst Militia opened fire as they passed by the church. In the first volley George Kingsmill – brother to Thomas – was shot and mortally wounded. The gang fired back, but randomly into buildings and into thin air. The militia fired to increasing good effect into their ranks. Two more were killed and many wounded – all on the Hawkhurst side – before they fled, pursued into the fields thereabouts by the men of Goudhurst brandishing cutlasses, swords, bill-hooks pitch-forks and the like.

It made Kingsmill and his men a deal more circumspect about venturing into Goudhurst in future, or into Cranbrook which had also formed its own militia. But it made him no more sensible when it came to planning expeditions. I have writ already of the ride to Poole to retake the tea captured off a smuggling cutter. But I have yet to make account of the events that took place thereafter, which resulted with the foul murders of Daniel Chater and William Galley, changed forever the opinion of the public about the trade in untaxed goods, and led to the demise of the Hawkhurst Gang, the execution of Staymaker Kingsmill, and in no small part to my own parlous predicament.

§§§§§

The journey back from Poole with the recaptured tea was like a triumphal procession. We rode in broad daylight through villages, and men women and children turned out to watch us and, in some cases, cheer us on. Having stopped for breakfast at Fordingbridge, on the edge of the New Forest to the south of Salisbury, one of our number fell into conversation with a local man. It seemed that John Dimmer, who had been with us on the Poole raid, was acquainted with a shoemaker from the village, one Daniel Chater. They'd helped bring in the harvest together in summers past and accounted themselves old friends. Thus, before parting, Dimmer shook Chater by the hand and passed him a parcel of tea. There was nothing so unusual in this, though perhaps to hand over untaxed goods in broad daylight in front of many witnesses was unwise. It certainly turned out so. But at the time we thought nothing of the incident and continued on our way to Hawkhurst where we unloaded and distributed the rest of the tea and went about our daily business.

But, back in Fordingbridge, Daniel Chater's continued bragging about his friendship with one of the Owlers reached the ears of the authorities. Still mightily angered by the audacious raid on the Poole Customs House and determined to have some revenge, they thereupon arrested John Dimmer and confined him at Chichester gaol and told the hapless Chater he was to be the key witness at the trial. Instead of being mightily afeared for his own safety, the foolish cobbler now started boasting about the role he was to have in helping to bring a smuggler to justice.

But if Chater was foolish, it was nothing to the sheer incompetence and idiocy of the Revenue themselves. They had to get Chater from Salisbury to Chichester in order for him formally to identify Diamond. Now you would have thought that so important a witness might be accorded the protection of a Platoon of Dragoons, or at very least several well-armed Revenue Officers. But no, they chose for his escort a single, elderly and equally foolish man named William Galley who was a tide waiter at Southampton – that's to say a minor employee of the Customs Service who rummages about in legitimate ships looking for any untaxed goods that might be concealed aboard.

Furthermore, they provided Galley with a large and official letter addressed to a Chichester magistrate outlining the entire business. On St Valentine's Day Seventeen-Forty-Eight, they dispatched him and Chater off on a journey from which neither would return.

§§§§§

I do not seek to defend what happened to Galley and Chater and in particular I do abhor the manner in which it occurred. But you must remember this was all in the context of the damned Indemnity Laws, and the fear of informers. I knew nothing of the events that unfolded on the first part of their journey until much later, and the story is usually told from the view of the Customs man and his witness, but I would seek to offer another perspective.

Imagine yourself Widow Payne, the innkeeper at the *White Hart* in Rowland's Castle. Two men dressed in their Sunday best on expensive horses ride up and as she serves them vittles and drink she overhears them discussing the Revenue Service and Magistrates and the Customs House affair. What should she do? She should inform her sons and friends and neighbours, free-traders all, in case the men's mission concerns them.

So in my view she is entirely justified in locking the stable door and pretending to have lost the keys to delay their departure. One son fetches the two Williams - Jackson and Carter. On questioning the travellers, they hear Chater say he is being 'obliged' to give evidence, and Galley proclaiming he is 'a King's officer'. Still wise counsel prevails and the two are given the hospitality of the inn and copious drink and they fall asleep. What more natural now for the Rowlands Castle lot to look among their possessions and, on discovering the official letter, to open and read it? Forget not that under the law now only the slightest suspicion of smuggling could be enough to send a man to the gallows.

So the two Williams find that Galley, and to a lesser extent Chater, are embarked on a course which would lead poor John

Dimmer to dance the hempen jig. What should they do? Why they should prevent the two men from reaching Chichester with the letter. Perhaps an excess of drink had been taken. Perhaps the exhortation of their womenfolk, afeared for their safety, swayed them overly. As I say I do not condone their tying Galley and Chater to their mounts and whipping them along the way. But even the official account concedes that once the men had slipped off the saddle and were suspended under the belly of the horse, its hooves kicking them in the head at every step, their captors untied them, and set them on other mounts behind the Rowlands Castle men.

I own that things did go to the worse from then on. And once they had reached the *Red Lion* at Rake, the Seacocks and Chichester men seemed quite out of control. But they had the presence of mind to send for others who had rode with the Hawkhurst gang and I account myself lucky to have declined the invitation. Having lately returned from the long ride to and from Poole, I was not anxious to set out on another expedition especially as my horse was lame and needed rest.

*William Galley and Daniel Chater whipped as
they fall from their horse*

*William Galley buried 'alive' at Harting Coombe*

The problem was they lacked an effective leader. Much of the indignities and ill-usage meted out to Galley and Chater was, I believe, due to indecision rather than sheer barbarity. Though I own that when retold in the court, barbarity seemed the better name for it. Anyhows, you have probably now read of how the captives were battered and bruised from their journey up from Rowlands Castle, and how William Galley seemed to have passed on. I, myself, do not believe the tale that he was still alive when they buried him. There is little evidence for the accusation save that when he was exhumed his hand was found to be over his eyes. That could be for divers reasons other than he was trying to keep the sand from off his face as they shovelled it into to his grave.

Keeping the injured Chater chained up in an outbuilding for two or three days and February nights, all the while whipping and beating him does seem a little unkind, as does the cutting off of his face, the unsuccessful attempt at hanging him and then the thrusting him down the well and throwing rocks upon him until his cries ceased. It is not the way I would have conducted business were I in charge. But then, as I say, I was not there. Or anywhere near. And my name does not appear in any of the accounts of the events. So you may take it that, on this occasion at least, I was entirely innocent. Though I cannot in all conscience say that I mourn overly for the departed Galley and Chater. Perhaps just for the manner of their going.

§§§§§

*Daniel Chater, chained and tortured by Smugglers*

Through my tiny window in the Norwich gaol I see a glimmer of light in the east. It presages the dawn and with it my forthcoming departure from this life and I must hasten to complete my tale. But in truth there is not much else to tell. After the deaths of Galley and Chater, life became extremely uncomfortable in the villages along the Kent and Sussex border and into Hampshire. Officers of the law knocked at many a home and offered copious sums of money for any information concerning the whereabouts of the missing men. It was not many months 'ere they received an anonymous letter disclosing the resting place of Galley's body. Then the traitorous William Steel turned King's Evidence and the whole house of cards crumbled. By the end of Seventeen-Forty-Eight, seven of the men involved had been arrested and, within a six month, divers others involved in the raid on the Poole Customs House were also under lock and key, including Staymaker Kingsmill and other leaders of the Hawkhurst 'gentlemen'. I was not among them, having taken myself back to London where I eked a living putting one man in touch with another to help a few lbs of tea move along the chain from importer to consumer.

Now think of me what you will, but accept please that I have been nothing if not candid in retelling the adventures of my life. I have held little back and if I have done so it is only to save the good name of others. So when I say to you now that I had nothing to do with robbing the Bedford mail, you will have to make up your own mind as to whether or not you believe me. What I will say is that a rogue by the name of John Jetter knows the truth of the matter as he was there, and held the horses behind a hedge while two others of his acquaintance held up and robbed the coach. I was in a tavern in

56

Southwark when the robbery occurred. But Jetter is about as trustworthy as a snake in the grass, and was in the mire so deep that he would have implicated his grandmother to avoid transportation or the gallows. So my name was given and a description eventually issued:

> "Whereas certain Information has been made upon Oath, before one of his Majesty's Justices of the Peace that the Chester Mail of 2nd July last was robbed by a Person who goes, or has gone by the several Names of GABRIEL TOMKINS alias YOUNG GIBB: alias KIT JERVIS, alias CHRISTOPHER WOOD, alias UNKLE, alias RAWLINS, who has been formerly a Smugler and was some Years since employed as a Riding Surveyor in the Service of the Customs and some Years ago lived at the Town of Dartford, in the County of Kent. He is a Man of between Forty and Fifty Years of Age, of a very swarthy Complexion, somewhat marked with the Small Pox, about Five Foot Nine or Ten Inches high, is a very well made Man, walks very upright, with large dark Eyebrows, which hang over his Eyes, and has formerly received a bullet Wound, in his Left Arm with a Pistol or Musquet Bullet, of which some Mark or Appearance is left. ... the above described Gabriel Tomkins has a small Wart or Wen at the corner of one of his Eye-brows, next to his Nose, and is said to appear in a shabby brown duffil Coat, much pieced and torn, and trimmed with white metal Buttons, a deep blue Waistcoat, and an old light or lightish Wig turned Yellow with the Wearing.

> "A Suitable Reward is hereby offered, and will be given to any Person or Persons, who shall apprehend a Woman, who goes or has gone by the several Names of Anne Hocks,

*alias Hawkswell, alias Matthews. She is a*
*Person of between Thirty and Forty Years*
*of Age, of a fair Complexion, and about*
*Five Foot Six Inches high, somewhat pitted*
*with the Small Pox, and has the letters*
*A.H. prick'd in upon one of her Hands with*
*Indian Ink or Gunpowder, and it is*
*supposed she does now, or has lately*
*accompanied Gabriel Tomkins above*
*described."*

As you will see, I managed to evade arrest on this charge for some three years, but eventually my luck ran out and I was taken to Newgate and thence to Bedford, tried in the most farcical manner for a crime I had not committed, and sentenced to death, the charges running thus:

*"Gabriel Tomkins, alias Young Gibb, alias*
*Kitt Jervis, alias Christopher Wood, alias*
*Unkle, alias Rawlins. For robbing Thomas*
*Roone in a certain field and open place near*
*King's Highway, and stole one Gray*
*Gelding, price £30 of Samuel Lord and*
*goods value £40 of our Lord the King."*

Other, lesser, men might rail against this miscarriage of justice but I look at it thuswise. Though I may be innocent of the Bedford Mail robbery I have, I now freely admit, stopped other coaches on the King's highway and robbed the travellers therein. And, as you know, I have taken part in many a landing of untaxed goods over near half a century. And I continued the practice of smuggling even when in the employment of the King as a Revenue Officer and Bailiff. So I cannot complain overmuch that I have been misused. Indeed the only

58

surprise is that I got away with it for so long. I still believe that the Government is foolish in imposing such swingeing duties on goods imported into this island and it will only been when such duties are removed altogether that smuggling with cease. But I am tired now. I have ridden through so many dark nights; hauled tubs through the breakers on so many freezing beaches; loaded and led so many ponies along the byways of Kent and Sussex; secreted them in so many lonely farmhouses; and fought off so many King's men that my end will come as a rest and a relief. I do not know quite how old I am. Certainly fifty and probably more. It has been a long and exciting life, and one I would not have changed. But it has been uncertain. Perhaps I would have been better off sticking to my trade as a bricklayer. Working assiduously day in day out putting a little aside, marrying a local girl and raising a family. But then I would have missed the thrill of saddling my horse at midnight and setting off down to the pounding shore, watching for the winking light of the sloop, and knowing the goods were on their way.

I repent that I did harm to some men, but not that I followed the course I set myself. I go from this cell to meet my maker unafraid of what lies ahead, and will not be sad if all my gravestone reads is:

## *Here Lies Gabriel Tomkins*
## *- Smuggler.*

# Acknowledgements

I would particularly like to thank John Dawes for his invaluable help in bringing this project to fruition, and to recommend his excellent reprint of 'Smugglers Murders' - the 1749 account of the killing of Galley and Chater which did so much to vilify the Hawkhurst Gang. I am also grateful to Herbert 'Tom' Browning for his help and painstaking research into the Gang and local smuggling in the 18th century, and to Simon Newman for drawing the maps. Many other people have been very generous with their time and assistance, including John Belknap, Celia Ellacott, Martin Lloyd, Kevin Crisman and the Lake Champlain Maritime Museum, June Holmes and the Natural History Society of Northumbria, and The Hawkhurst Community Partnership. I am indebted to a large number of historians and writers on smuggling including Paul Muskett, Mary Waugh, Richard Platt, FF Nichols and John Douch.

Ultimately though, the person who made this book possible is Gabriel Tomkins himself. He managed to get his name into the official records of nearly three centuries ago far more often than most of his smuggling contemporaries. This has enabled me to piece together a reasonable narrative of his life story. I trust that wherever he is now he will forgive me for having taken a few liberties in filling in the gaps!

I would be delighted to hear from anyone who knows more about Tomkins or his family.

KB

*Email: Publishing@KentBarker.Co.Uk*